Don't Step in the Trap!

How to Recognize and Avoid Email Phishing Scams

. . . In Plain English

BRETT W. SMITH

ISBN: 1534765026
ISBN-13: 978-1534765023

CONTENTS

Introduction

IT WAS LATE in the afternoon on Tuesday. The sun shone through the third-floor window, creating a glare on the computer screen. Kyle got up from his desk and adjusted the window blinds. As he sat down, he turned back to the monthly reports he was running for the management meeting in the morning. As an assistant in the accounting department, it was his job to get the reports ready. Some of the reports were done in Excel, and others were run from the new accounting system that the company had switched to eight weeks before. A few still had to be pulled from the legacy system, which was still in use for some accounts while the bugs were being worked out of the new program. It was very time-consuming. Kyle always ended up working late the afternoon before the management meetings. It would be worse than usual today, because he also had to find time to upload the monthly invoice into their biggest customer's online system.

It didn't help that his workstation hadn't been upgraded yet. Running reports in the new accounting system seemed to take forever. At the year-end company meeting, the owner had announced that the older workstations were to be replaced once the revenue had been booked from the completion of the work on the new shopping mall. Kyle was very much looking forward to that happening in the next quarter. Judging by the reports he had prepared so far, it looked like it was going to be a good year.

As he waited for a report to come up, Kyle saw that an email had come in from the IT department with the subject of "Admin Notice." He opened it, and read that his Outlook mailbox had exceeded its storage limit. The email instructed him on what to do to increase the limit. Following the directions, he clicked on the link included in the email, put in his username and password, and hit submit. Once that was done, he deleted the email, and went back to his reports. It was going to be a long afternoon.

He didn't realize that he had just given his username and password to data thieves. He also didn't know that by the end of the year, the company name was going to be in the news, connected to a massive data breach at their biggest customer, a national retail store chain. Losses from the breach, not to mention the damage to the company's reputation, were going to be serious. It wouldn't be a good year after all.

Chapter One –
What Is Phishing?

The story you just read was fictionalized. However, a similar event resulted in a data breach at Target in 2013 in which personal information of 70 million consumers was stolen, along with 40 million credit card numbers. As a result, Target reportedly faced potential losses of $1 billion. Investigations into the breach showed that one or more employees of a third-party Target vendor had been the victims of an email scam. The vendor, Fazio Mechanical Services, Inc., had access to an online Target system for vendors, used for the purpose of submitting invoices, contracts, and other documents. As a result of the scam, the vendor's network credentials were stolen. Once the scammers accessed Target's vendor system with those credentials, they were able to break through to other Target systems to steal credit card numbers and other customer information.

The type of scam that was used to steal the vendor's network credentials is called **phishing**. The U.S. Federal

Bureau of Investigation defines "phishing" as "the act of sending an email falsely claiming to be [from] an established legitimate business in an attempt to dupe the unsuspecting recipient into divulging personal, sensitive information."

In one example of a phishing attack, emails which claimed to be from credit card companies instructed consumers to verify their personal information in order to receive one of the new chip-enabled credit cards. If the consumers were unwary enough to provide the requested information, they were at risk of identity theft. If they clicked on links in the email, they likely had malicious software installed on their computers designed to steal information from them.

Basically, phishing is a trick, designed to take something of value from you. In simple terms, it is a trap. When exterminators put out a mousetrap to catch a mouse, they hope the mouse will be greedy or careless enough to only see the cheese, and that it won't notice the spring mechanism poised to take its life. Similarly, scammers hope to mislead us into triggering the trap they have set, poised to take valuable information from us, which they can then use to steal from us further.

Phishing attacks can come in a variety of ways. We typically think of emails being involved, and we will look at some examples of such emails later. However, attacks can also be delivered by text messaging. Since the formal name for text messaging is SMS (for Short Message Service), such attacks are referred to as **smishing**.

Some scammers use smishing schemes to defeat email password protection systems. In these schemes, they first obtain their potential victim's email address and cell phone number. Then they click on the "Forgot My Password" link at the email login screen, and select the option to have a code texted to the victim's cell phone. Next, they text the victim themselves, say that they are from the email provider and that the email account has been hacked, and ask the victim to reply with the verification code that just came through. Once the victim texts them the code, the scammers can reset the password for the email account and then have full control over it.

Similarly, scams perpetrated through phone calls (by voice) are called **vishing**.

Vishing schemes can start with a typical phishing email, but instead of including directions to click on a link, the email will instruct the recipient to call a phone number. When victims call the number, they are asked to provide their account number and password, thus turning that information over to the criminals. Alternatively, a vishing attack can happen with the scammer calling the victim directly to trick the person into providing sensitive information.

Most phishing scams used to be sent out in a "scattershot" fashion to as many potential victims as possible. Thus, when you received an email from a bank you didn't have an account with asking you to confirm your account information, it was easy to conclude that the email was a scam. However, the attacks have now become more sophisticated. In fact, 91% of phishing attacks are now highly targeted, in a category called **spear phishing**. In these attacks, the fraudsters first gather information about their potential victim in order to customize the phishing email to make it more believable.

This is illustrated by an attack some years ago on AT&T customers. Hackers had broken into the company's systems and were able to steal detailed information on customers, including names, addresses, order information, and credit card numbers. They then sent customized emails to each customer, referencing their particular order, claiming that there was a problem with the order. Customers were instructed that they could resolve the problem by going to a website and entering personal information, including their birthdates and social security numbers. Of course, the website was a fake (a "spoofed" version of a real AT&T website), and the customers who entered their personal information were likely later victims of identity theft.

When spear phishing attacks are directed to senior executives or celebrities using careful research, such attacks are called **whaling**.

In one whaling scam, the chief financial officer at a large company received an email ostensibly from the chief executive officer instructing him to transfer $192,000 to a foreign bank account. The scammers had determined who in the company made such transfers, and drafted the email to be very convincing. It contained no telltale clues to indicate it was a fake. Fortunately in that instance, when the CFO contacted the CEO to ask for the purpose of the transfer, the scam was discovered before any money was lost. Other companies have not been as lucky. The Federal Bureau of Investigation indicated that around 1,200 companies or individuals had lost a total of over $179 million to this kind of scam during only three months in 2014.

To do their research, the cybercriminals often use a method called **social engineering**, which is to use basic social skills and psychological manipulation to gather information about a person, an organization, or its computer network. For example, they might impersonate someone from the phone company or the IT department to first get some basic information about the accounting department from a receptionist, then use that information to get additional details from someone in the accounting department, then impersonate someone in the accounting department to get more sensitive information from a manager, and so on. Alternatively, they might use information from social media to figure out what an employee is interested in, and then they would use that information to prepare a targeted, enticing phishing email. Some criminals even manage to gain physical access to offices by impersonating delivery people, or by duping an employee into letting them through a secured access point without a badge, which they supposedly forgot.

No matter what type of attack is involved, they all have one thing in common: they all try to trick you into getting caught in a trap, so that they can take something of value from you. Our best defense is to be able to recognize the trap before stepping into it.

Chapter Two –
Is Phishing a Serious Problem?

Typically, when we worry about hackers breaking into our computer systems, we focus on whether our software and operating systems are all up to date, with all the latest security patches installed. Unfortunately for us, however, it has been estimated that only about 3% of cyber attacks involve hackers attempting to exploit "holes" in our systems. Most attacks (about 97%) involve attempts to dupe their victims into falling for phishing schemes or something similar.

Phishing attacks have become a significant threat. Consider the following numbers:

- 156 million phishing emails are sent out every day.
- Email users receive up to 20 phishing emails each month.
- On average, it only takes 82 seconds from the time a phishing email is first distributed until the first victim is hooked.

- One study revealed that 23% of recipients open phishing emails.
- That study also found that 11% of recipients also open the malicious attachments. In a different study, over 25% clicked on fraudulent links.
- Websites connected to phishing attacks were able to steal information from between 3% to 45% of their visitors, depending on the particular site.
- Within 30 minutes of a phishing attack, 20% of user accounts were compromised.
- Total losses from phishing attacks in a single year (2013) were estimated at $5.9 billion.
- 91% of reported data breaches resulted from phishing schemes.
- The average large company loses $4 million every year to phishing attacks.

Some attacks result in much larger losses. In addition to the Target attack mentioned before, another high-profile data breach resulting from an initial phishing attack was the 2014 cyber break-in at Sony Pictures Entertainment, later attributed to the North Korean government. Initially, Sony executives received phishing emails requesting their Apple IDs and passwords supposedly for verification purposes. The scammers ultimately managed to use the information obtained through the attack to successfully compromise Sony's servers. As a result of this attack, a massive amount of confidential Sony information was publicly released. Sony's costs for investigation and remediation alone were reported at about $15 million. In addition, claims against Sony from its employees and former employees for the theft of their personal information (such as social security numbers) were later settled for as much as $8 million. Other losses were undoubtedly even higher.

What kind of losses can we face from phishing?

Money: After an employee of Penneco Oil Company, Inc., fell victim to a phishing attack in 2012, hackers transferred over $3.5 million from the corporate bank accounts to banks in Russia and Belarus.

Trade secrets: In addition to cash, hackers also steal trade secrets. For example, some attacks have been focused on law firms, in an effort to reach clients' intellectual property and other confidential information. A loss of a company's trade secrets could be devastating to a company's competitive position in the marketplace.

Personal information: Information relating to about 2,800 individuals, including birthdates and social security numbers, was exposed to theft in September 2015, when an employee of North Oldham High School in Kentucky was duped into accessing a malicious website. Similarly, in March 2016, copies of federal Form W-2 for several thousand employees, containing social security numbers and payroll information, were forwarded to scammers, when a Seagate Technology employee was fooled by a fraudulent email that appeared to be a request from upper management.

Computer files: One hacker stole login information from a large number of celebrities by sending them emails claiming to be from Google or Apple. With that information, he accessed their email and iCloud accounts, and was able to download files, videos, and photos, including nude photos. Later, their nude photos appeared on the internet, causing the victims considerable embarrassment and emotional distress.

Identify theft: Criminals often use the information they obtain through phishing for identity theft. In one 2012 case, an individual was convicted in federal court for using information stolen in a phishing attack to withdraw funds from bank accounts and to create counterfeit driver's licenses. With such licenses and other information, criminals can open new credit accounts in the victim's name, wreaking havoc with the victim's credit history.

Having computer files held for ransom: Some victims opened a document attached to an email which they thought was from the Internal Revenue Service, thinking it related to their tax refund. Instead, the file encrypted the contents of their hard drives. Only by paying a ransom could they get their files unlocked. Similarly, in February 2016, Hollywood Presbyterian Medical Center paid a $17,000 ransom to have its computer files unlocked after such an attack.

Significant response costs: The costs a business incurs in responding to a data breach can be substantial. Typically, security consultants and lawyers must be engaged to investigate and respond to the breach. In addition to the costs of a forensic investigation and any remedial steps, at least forty-six states and certain municipalities require companies to notify individuals whose personal information has been compromised. Compiling lists of those affected and sending out such notices can take a great deal of time and effort. Notices may also need to be sent to government agencies, the media, and credit reporting agencies. Moreover, credit monitoring, identity theft insurance, or other such services may need to be purchased for the customers or other individuals whose information was compromised. A 2013 study of data breaches involving no more than 100,000 customer records concluded that the average cost of a breach that year was $5.8 million. That amount included response costs and the loss of business due to damage to firms' reputations.

Business disruption: At the very least, when a data breach occurs as a result of a phishing attack, a company and its personnel will be distracted from their regular business by the need to investigate the breach, close down any "holes" in their systems being exploited by attackers, determine the identities of those whose personal information may have been compromised, provide required notices, deal with customer, employee, and media inquiries, repair systems as needed, restore data from backups, change passwords, update or revise security protocols, and train personnel to try to prevent another such incident. To the extent that computer systems need to isolated or taken offline as a result of a breach, or if data has been permanently lost, the short-term disruption to a company's business could be much more serious. In addition, government and media investigations and legal claims may cause significant long-term distractions.

Other business losses: Businesses can suffer additional losses which are more difficult to quantify. These include reduced employee morale, loss of customers, lost sales, loss of profits, and loss of business reputation. For example, in a 2014 survey, 28% of businesses which had been the subject of a phishing attack reported that the reputation of the business had been damaged. In addition, upon the announcement of a data breach resulting from phishing, public companies may suffer a downturn in their stock price.

Claims for identify theft: Individuals whose personal information was lost to scammers in a data breach at a company have sued the company to recover the cost of their efforts to reduce the risk of identity theft.

Claims for inappropriate disclosure of medical information: If a hospital or medical practice is victimized by a phishing attack and thereby loses patient data, the patient may have a claim under state law for the failure to safeguard their data.

Federal penalties for unfair or deceptive practices: The Federal Trade Commission (FTC) seeks to ensure that companies live up to their claims that they protect consumers' information, and can sue companies which do not do so. Thus, if a company falls victim to a phishing attack which results in the loss of consumers' personal information, the FTC may file suit, claiming that the company misled consumers by failing to maintain the security of the information.

Fines under state privacy laws: Many states have laws allowing them to sue businesses for violations of their laws relating to data privacy and security. For instance, Texas law provides for civil penalties for failing to safeguard personal information and for failing to provide proper notice of data breaches, totaling up to $300,000.

Civil penalties under the Health Insurance Portability and Accountability Act (HIPAA): HIPAA is federal legislation governing data privacy and the security of personal health information. It provides for civil penalties (fines) for violations. When we consider that a 2015 study found that the health care industry was 74% more likely than average to be affected by phishing attacks, we see that there is a significant potential for health care providers to be victims of the theft of their patients' personal health information, and thus subject to HIPAA fines. As an example, in December 2015, the University of Washington Medicine settled HIPAA claims with the U.S. Department of Health and Human Services for $750,000. The claims arose out of the compromise of the information of 90,000 individuals after a university employee opened a link in a phishing email.

Litigation expenses: Even if a company wins a case and does not have to pay claims such as those above, they still have to pay their lawyers to defend them and cover other costs, all of which add up quickly.

Chapter Three –
How Do We Recognize a Phishing Scam?

The basic rule to keep from falling into a phishing trap is to check before you step, or in other words, check before you click.

There are six basic elements in an email to check:

- From:
- To:
- Subject
- Attachments
- Content
- Hyperlinks

In the following chapters, we will review each of these elements in detail.

Chapter Four –
Who is Sending the Email?

When you look at an email, first check the "From:" field. You might see the word "From," or, more likely, you will just see information about the sender at the top of the message. There are two items of information you can find in this field: the sender's name and the sender's email address.

Obviously, fraudsters will not send out phishing emails using their own names or email addresses. Instead, they will steal someone else's information or they may make something up. They might use the name of someone you know or of a company you do business with.

Different email websites or programs (called "clients") will show the name and email address of the sender in different ways. They may display only the person's name so that you have to move your cursor over the name to have the email address pop up, or the address may show up in a sidebar, or they may show the name and the address together. On a mobile device, you may have to tap the sender's name to see the associated properties, including the email address.

As you probably already know, email addresses are formatted to show a person's name or identifier, followed by the @ symbol, and then the name of the email service, company, or website which hosts the email account (called the "domain name"). Thus, if someone had the email address of john@gmail.com, "gmail.com" is the domain name.

To identify a fraudulent email, watch for discrepancies in the From: field.

One type of discrepancy is misspellings. For example, a message may claim to be from PayPal but the sender's domain name is shown as *paypall.com*. Or a domain name may be cleverly misspelled so that it resembles a legitimate domain name. An example of this is as putting certain letters in the name together so that they look like another letter at first glance, such as using "rn" instead of "m" (like *bankofarnerica.com*). Alternatively, there may be misspellings in the sender's name itself. Improper capitalization can also be a clue.

Another discrepancy to watch for is a domain name in the email address that doesn't match the supposed seller. For example, if eBay is going to send you an email, it will come from someone at *ebay.com*. If you receive an email from someone with a domain like *ebay.cix55.com*, that could well be a scam. In that case, the actual domain name is "cix55.com" and the "ebay" in the name is really meaningless.

You can also watch for domain names that look like gibberish instead of a legitimate company name or website.

One obvious clue that an email is a phishing attack is when you see that the name and the email address do not match. For example, the phishing email reproduced in Figure 1 shows "western University" as the sender, but the email address is from a different institution.

Figure 1

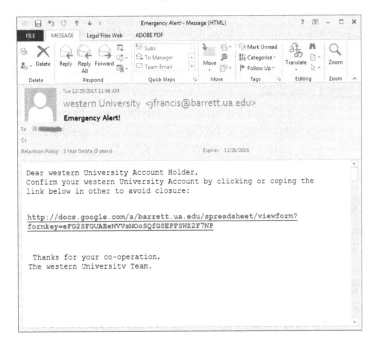

Another red flag to watch for in the business context is an email supposedly from a top-level manager where the domain name is not connected with the company. This is typical of phishing messages containing urgent requests for sensitive business-related information (like a copy of all employees' W-2 forms).

Finally, you should always be wary when receiving emails from people you don't know.

In summary, if something is not right with the information in the From: line, that is an obvious red flag. Unfortunately, however, email addresses can be forged, so the address and the associated sender's name might look fine.

There is more to check.

Chapter Five –
Who Was the Email Sent To?

Another part of an email which you should check is the To: field.

First, let me provide a little background explanation. When we write an email, we usually select the recipient's name from the address book, or it is filled in by way of an "autocomplete" entry, or we manually type in the recipient's email address. After that, we see the recipient's name or email address in the To: field of our draft message.

However, there are other ways that a recipient can be included on a message. One way is by using the cc: ("carbon copy") field. This field works in the same way as the To: field, except that the recipient's name or email address will show up next to "cc:" instead of next to "To:". Otherwise, a recipient who receives a "carbon copy" of an email won't see anything different than a recipient who receives an "original," since we aren't using actual carbon paper for copies any more.

There is also a bcc: ("blind carbon copy") field. It also works in the same way as the To: field, with one exception: The names and addresses of recipients listed in the bcc: field will not be visible. Consequently, if a message is sent to John Smith, with a cc: to Mary Jones, and a bcc: to Bob Williams, John and Mary will see each other's names or email addresses, but neither of them will see Bob's. Bob will see John and Mary's information, but he won't see his own, either. If a message is sent as a bcc: to all three of them, with no one listed in the To: or cc: fields, then none of them will see any information on recipients (or, depending on the particular email system, they might see something in the To: field like "undisclosed-recipients").

Finally, if a sender wants to send a message to multiple people at once, instead of typing in individual email addresses, the sender could create an email group. This is typically done by creating an entry in the address book with multiple email addresses shown under a single name describing the group. Depending on the email system, if the group is added to the To: or cc: fields, recipients of messages sent to the group will see either the group name or the names or email addresses of the various members of the group.

One normal feature of legitimate emails is that the list of recipients makes sense in some way. In addition, businesses, government agencies, and other organizations are typically careful to safeguard the personal information of the people they communicate with. So, for example, when you get an email from your financial institution, you should only see your own name or email address in the To: field, if anything is shown at all.

Therefore, a clue that an email is not legitimate can be found in how the recipients are listed. If you see a list of multiple recipients in the To: field of a message containing personal information which was apparently sent by a business or other organization, that can be an indication that the message is a phishing email.

Another indication is an email which was sent to multiple recipients who are apparently unrelated. See the phishing email reproduced in Figure 2 for an example.

Figure 2

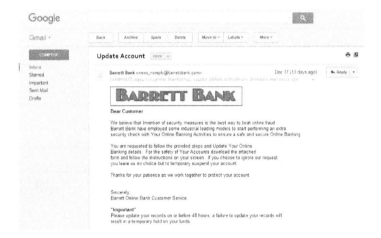

It can also be suspicious when a message is sent to an odd grouping of recipients, such as people whose names start with the same letter but who are not otherwise connected.

Remember that, generally, the sender of a legitimate email about an important subject won't send it in a way that the various recipients can see each other's email addresses. In addition, such a sender will make the email specific to each recipient. If an email violates these principles, it may well be a phishing scam.

Unfortunately, scammers are getting more sophisticated, so not all phishing emails will leave clues in the To: field. Again, there is more to check.

Chapter Six –
Is Something Attached to the Message?

When you send an email to someone, you have the option of attaching one or more documents or other computer files. This can be a handy method for delivering documents, photos, and other files to an email recipient. However, when you receive an email with an attachment, that can be an indication that the email is not legitimate.

As a general rule, email attachments should not be trusted, even if they are sent by someone you know. Why not? Because you never know when someone else's computer may have been compromised. Of course, as with any general rule, there are exceptions.

First, if you are expecting to receive the particular attachment, then such an email is less likely to be a scam.

Second, if the attached file has a ".txt" extension, it should be safe to open (if you are sure you are looking at the real extension of the file). So what is an extension?

The extension of a file is the part of the file name at the very end after the period, typically three letters. It indicates the type of the file. So, for example, a file name which ends in ".doc" is understood to be a Microsoft Word document, while an ".xls" file would be a Microsoft Excel spreadsheet. A few other examples are ".jpg" for a common format for a photo or other image file, ".pdf" for an Adobe Acrobat Portable Document Format file, ".exe" for an executable file (a computer program), and ".txt" for a plain text file.

Files with the ".txt" extension are safe to open; any other file type can contain malicious code.

Nevertheless, caution is still warranted. Scammers often try to fool us by taking advantage of a couple of features of our computer systems which were designed to be of benefit to us.

One of these features is that commonly-used computer operating systems (including both Windows and Mac) are often set up to hide file extensions by default. There are a variety of reasons for this. For one, these graphical operating systems typically use easily recognizable file icons for particular file types. A user may wish to reduce screen clutter by hiding file extensions, since they can tell what kind of a file it is by glancing at the file icon. Another reason is that changing file extensions may cause instability or make files more difficult to open, and when the file extension is hidden, it is more difficult to change.

The second of these features is our ability to give a file a long file name. When personal computers were new, the MS-DOS operating system which was used at the time required users to limit their file names to eight characters followed by a period and the three-letter file extension. It could be a big headache for users to try to remember what cryptic eight-letter name they used for any particular file, so it was a great improvement when the programmers gave us the ability to use file names that were much longer. In our long file names, in addition to letters of the alphabet, we can use various special characters, like the underscore (_) symbol, hyphen, brackets, percent sign (%), exclamation point, tilde (~), comma, and period, among others.

Someone with malicious intent can use those features to try to trick us. Here is an example. Let's say that we have a virus-infected executable file (a file with the ".exe" extension) that we want to fool someone into opening. We might then name it something like "Funny picture", but a file name of "Funny picture.exe" would likely look suspicious. However, since we can include a period in the file name, there is nothing to stop us from naming the file "Funny picture.jpg.exe". If we do that, then any user whose system hides file extensions by default will only see "Funny picture.jpg". They might be fooled into thinking that the file was only a ".jpg" photo file, and not notice that it is actually an ".exe" executable file.

Thus, a scammer could put ".txt" at the end of a file name, before the real extension, in an effort to trick us into thinking that the file was a safe plain text file. For this reason, we should only assume that a ".txt" file is safe if we are sure that that is the actual extension of the file.

Whenever we see a file that appears to have a double extension (like "document.txt.zip"), we should treat that as a definite "red flag" warning us that the file is likely to be infected or malicious.

By the way, to improve your chances of not being fooled by a fake file extension, it is recommended that you adjust the settings for your operating system so that file extensions are not hidden. How to do that will depend on your particular operating system. A simple way to figure that out is to do a Google search for "how to unhide file extensions in *(insert your particular operating system)*" and then follow the instructions you find.

Chapter Seven –
What is the Subject Line of the Email?

When we send an email to someone, we want to make sure they actually see it and open it. We are all bombarded by so many emails each day that it is easy for important or interesting messages to get buried. One tool we have to make sure our messages are noticed is the subject line of the message. Fraudsters particularly would like us to open their emails, so they often use the subject line of the message to draw our attention.

They know that one way to entice us to open their messages is to appeal to our emotions, such as fear, greed or curiosity. For this reason, we should be on our guard when we see email subject lines which convey a sense of urgency, cause us apprehension, or tempt us with something illicit.

Here are a few examples, with samples of what the scammers want us to think:

- "Final reminder: Notice of Tax Return" – am I late on some required filing?

- "Service cancellation in 10 days" – is there something I need to renew?
- "Are you at your desk?" – does the boss need something in a hurry?
- "Notification of Personal Information Error" – is something wrong that I need to fix?
- "Notice of payment" – am I getting some money?
- "University Terror Alert***" – am I in danger?
- "Notice of appearance in court" – am I in legal trouble?
- "YOUR ACCOUNT HAS BEEN SUSPENDED !!!" – is there a problem with my bank account or credit card?
- "Urgent" – uh oh, what's up now? I'd better check.
- "Emergency Alert!" – what kind of emergency am I facing?
- "Congratulations, you won!" – great, what did I win?
- "You won't believe these photos" – hmm, I wonder what those look like?

If a phishing email is a trap, then the subject line of the email can be the bait, dangled in front of us in hopes that we will take it.

There are other clues in subject lines which can indicate that a message may be fraudulent. One is a subject that is very general, such as "Email Notification" or "Important Message".

Another is a subject line that does not match the content of a message you have opened. For example, if the subject line says "Investment Opportunity" but the content of the message is about something else entirely, that is an obvious red flag.

Yet another clue is a subject line that is strangely worded, uses inconsistent capitalization, or contains misspelled words.

An obvious example would be something like "To Restore Your Account Accses You must verfiy Your Information".

One further clue to look for requires a little explanation first. When we send an email, we can put in pretty much any subject line we want. When the recipient reads our email, he or she may want to reply. When the reply is sent, our computer systems typically insert the word "Re:" at the beginning of the subject line of the reply, followed by our original subject. Similarly, if the recipient forwards our email, the person to whom the email is forwarded will receive an email with "Fwd:" at the beginning of the subject line, followed by our original subject line. Of course, our recipient can always edit the subject line before the message is replied to or forwarded, but typically most of us just accept the usual defaults put in by our computer systems.

Consequently, when we receive an email with a subject line starting with "Re:", it is normal for us to expect that this is a reply to a message we sent. It is likely that we will open a reply to a message we sent. Scammers rely on this tendency by sending out fraudulent emails having subject lines starting with "Re:" followed by some wording. When we receive a message which appears to be a reply to a message we did not send, that is a red flag that the email may not be legitimate.

Chapter Eight –
What Does the Email Say?

The contents of emails can vary widely. Some phishing emails can be very convincing. Others are less so. Here are some patterns to watch for, when considering whether an email is legitimate or not.

First of all, if you receive an email that has very little or no content other than a hyperlink (an internet address you can click on that will take you to a website, download a document, or start a program), that is virtually always a scam of some sort. Don't click on the link!

Similarly, be very wary of emails with little or no content other than an attached file. As discussed in Chapter Six, email attachments should generally not be trusted, unless you are expecting to receive them.

The types of messages described above would likely seem suspicious. Other phishing emails try to lull victims into a false sense of security by copying corporate or government logos and formats which look familiar.

However, if an email which appears to have been sent by a financial institution or other organization you deal with is worded in a very general way (addressed, for example, only to "Valued Customer"), rather than being personalized to you, that would be a red flag. Typically, legitimate emails would be drafted to be customer-specific.

Another possible clue that an email may be a scam is when you receive one which appears to be a duplicate or a resend of a one you received before. One phishing trick which fraudsters use (called "clone phishing") is to gain access to a legitimate email and copy the content and formatting while substituting fraudulent links or attachments for any originals. They then send it out as a "correction" which appears to come from the original sender.

Next, many of the same considerations apply when looking at email contents as we reviewed in connection with email subject lines. Specifically, if the contents of a message convey an unusual sense of urgency, or appeal to emotions such as greed, fear, or curiosity, that is an indication that the message may be fraudulent. For example, phishing emails can make the message seem urgent by threatening recipients with dire consequences for failing to take the actions demanded by the message.

One phishing email which used fear as the bait to entice the victim to open the message and its attachment appeared to come from the victim's physician, stating that the attachment was a notice that the victim had been diagnosed with cancer. In another instance, an email appeared to come from a well-known law firm, claiming that the recipient had to appear in court, with the details supposedly being set forth in an attachment or accessible by clicking on a link.

Word choice, grammar, and spelling can also provide an indication that an email is not legitimate. Some scammers are from overseas and are not native speakers of American English, and thus tend to misspell words, or use odd phrasing, poor grammar, inappropriate punctuation, unusual capitalization, or make other such errors. This is a big red flag.

In summary, if something about the message just doesn't look or feel right, trust your instincts and be suspicious of the message.

Finally, if the message instructs you to open an attachment or click on a link, don't do it!

When you are looking at emails, there are certain general principles you can rely on.

First, financial institutions and other reputable entities will not contact you with a request that you provide your personal information, such as social security numbers, bank account details, or passwords. They already have that information on file. If there is some action they want you to take, they will direct you to login at their website, rather than directing you to click on a link or open an attachment. (Of course, if you initiate contact with them, they may ask for your account number or other identifying information in order to find you in their computer system.)

Similarly, government agencies such as the Federal Bureau of Investigation (FBI) and the Internal Revenue Service (IRS) do not send unsolicited emails to individuals. Moreover, courts do not use email to deliver official legal documents to individuals, such as notices to appear, subpoenas, and the like.

In one scam, an email supposedly from the IRS instructed recipients to provide information to verify their identity. While the IRS does send out identity verification forms by postal mail, they do not use email for that purpose.

In addition, financial institutions, email providers, and other well-known businesses will never threaten to freeze your account or suspend access to it unless you "verify" your information by some arbitrary, short deadline.

Never give out your user ID or password to any sensitive account, including your email account.

If you get a request to disclose personal information, transfer money, or take any other action that could result in the loss of something valuable, double-check before you do anything, even if the request appears legitimate. Don't rely on any contact information shown in the email; instead, look up the phone number or email address on your account statement, in published sources, or otherwise.

Another principle to remember is that legitimate enterprises are very careful to present a professional appearance. They have marketing and communications personnel trained to use proper English. Their personnel use correct spelling (or at least make good use of spell checkers), follow the rules of English grammar, and usually work hard to make their email messages understandable.

Messages that come from individuals should also be treated with caution. For example, emails that entice you to look at sensational photos, embarrassing images of celebrities, or free pornography, are very likely to be phishing scams.

If a Nigerian prince, American soldier, or some other stranger contacts you with a tale of a large amount of money which needs to be retrieved in secret, with you getting a hefty percentage with absolutely no risk, just delete the message. The old saying is still true: If the offer is "too good to be true," it probably is.

Similarly, if you get an email from friends or relatives who claim they are stranded in a foreign country, asking you to send them money, don't believe it, unless you knew beforehand that they were actually traveling to that location. In that case, you should make arrangements to contact them directly before you do anything else, so you can verify that the message really came from them.

Having discussed all of these principles, we must recognize the unfortunate fact that many scammers are getting more sophisticated. Phishing emails often look very convincing. Indicators which were previously common, such as those mentioned above, may no longer be present.

Despite that, we need not be discouraged. There is one last element we can check.

Chapter Nine –
Is There a Single Key to Recognizing Most Phishing Emails?

There is one thing that can be called the key to recognizing most phishing emails: hyperlinks.

A hyperlink is an image or a line of text which you can click on that will open a website or a document, or initiate some other action. Most hyperlinks are a line of text; the text of such a hyperlink can be the actual web address where it will take you (like "http://www.paypal.com/login"), or it can be some other wording (such as "Click here to open", with the word "here" being the hyperlink). By default, most computer systems will mark hyperlinks with underlining and a different color than the surrounding text, often blue.

Since you can use any text for a hyperlink, scammers will use what looks like a trusted web address for a hyperlink that leads somewhere else altogether. Consequently, a link like this:

"Click here to download form:
http://www.irs.gov/form1040.pdf"

could actually open a malicious file or website instead.

Fortunately, there is an easy way to tell what a hyperlink will do. Hover your cursor over the link *without* clicking on it. At that point, the default arrow cursor will change on most systems to a hand with the index finger outstretched. Your browser or email program will then show you where the link will take you, typically at the bottom left of the window or screen.

Mobile devices which have no mouse require a different approach. For example, on an iPad or iPhone, press and hold on the link to see a popup message which will show the address embedded in the link together with a menu of options.

If the address within the link doesn't match the message, is misspelled, or otherwise seems suspicious, it is undoubtedly malicious. It's a trap! Don't step in it!

Remember, however, that not all phishing emails contact hyperlinks. Consequently, an email is not necessarily safe just because it does not contain a hyperlink, or even when all of its hyperlinks are legitimate. Keep all the other principles in mind which have been discussed in previous chapters.

Chapter Ten –
So What Do I Do with This Phishing Email?

When you identify that an email is actually a phishing scam, you could just delete it. However, it is a better idea to do something with it to try to help stop the scammers. Here are some things you can do.

First, forward the email to spam@uce.gov. This will add the message to a database at the Federal Trade Commission (FTC). The FTC and law enforcement agencies use this database to support prosecutions of scammers.

You can also forward the email to reportphishing@antiphishing.org. This will send it to the database of the Anti-Phishing Working Group (APWG), a private international organization with members from the private and public sectors, including internet service providers, security companies, government agencies, and others. Their database is used by internet security companies and other researchers to study internet fraud and prepare countermeasures.

In addition, the United States Computer Emergency Readiness Team (US-CERT) of the Department of Homeland Security asks that phishing emails be forwarded to them at phishing-report@us-cert.gov. They use the information to help individuals keep from being victimized by phishing schemes.

Next, submit an online complaint with the Federal Bureau of Investigation's Internet Crime Complaint Center (IC3) at www.ic3.gov. Complaints can relate to actual or attempted crimes, so you don't need to have actually become a victim to file a complaint. While IC3 does not actually investigate or prosecute offenses, they serve as a clearinghouse, reviewing complaints and forwarding them on to other agencies for appropriate action.

If a hyperlink in a message would take you to a fraudulent website, you can easily report that website to Google. They will add it to their database of unsafe websites and warn other users who try to go to that site. Simply copy the link and paste it in Google's "Report Phishing" page at https://www.google.com/safebrowsing/report_phish/.

If the phishing email tries to dupe you into believing that it came from some reputable organization, you should forward it to that business or agency as well. Here is how to report it to some major entities:

ADP: Forward the email (as an attachment, if possible) to abuse@adp.com.

Apple: Forward the email (as an attachment, if possible) to reportphishing@apple.com.

AT&T: Forward the email to scam@abuse-att.net.

Bank of America: Forward the email to abuse@bankofamerica.com.

Better Business Bureau: Forward the email to phishing@council.bbb.org.

Chase Bank: Forward the email to abuse@chase.com.

Dropbox: Forward the email to abuse@dropbox.com.

Ebay: Forward the email to spoof@ebay.com.

Facebook: Forward the email to phish@fb.com.

Google: Report phishing emails sent from Gmail accounts by completing the form at https://support.google.com/mail/contact/abuse.

Internal Revenue Service: Forward the email to phishing@irs.gov.

Microsoft: Forward the email (as an attachment, if possible) to phish@office365.microsoft.com. Otherwise, leave the body of your message blank.

PayPal: Forward the email to spoof@paypal.com. Do not forward it as an attachment.

Verizon: Go to http://www.verizon.com/info/reportphishing/?c=2 and click on the "Submit Report" button.

Wells Fargo: Forward the email to reportphish@wellsfargo.com.

Remember that these addresses are only to report messages which purport to come specifically from these organizations. When you forward the email as described above, include the full email header if you are able to do so. If you don't know how to do that, you should be able to find instructions by doing a search for "forward full email headers" in the Help system for your email program. However, even if you just forward the message without worrying about the headers, that will still be helpful.

If the organization that the email appears to have come from is not in the above list, simply do a search in Google for "report phishing" and the name of the organization, and you should be able to find instructions for how to report it.

Often, you can also use tools within your browser or email program to report scams. Here are instructions on how to do so within various popular email programs:

iCloud Mail: Click on the message to select it, then click either on "Message" or "Actions" (depending on which menu your system displays), and click on "Forward as Attachment." Forward the message to abuse@icloud.com.

Gmail: Click on the small down arrow to the right of the "Reply" button at the top right of the message, and select "Report Phishing" from the menu that appears.

Outlook.com: In the menu above the subject line of the message, click on the small down arrow to the right of "Junk," and select "Phishing Scam" from the menu.

Outlook 2010 or 2013: Right-click on the email, click on Junk, then "Report Junk."

Yahoo Mail: In the menu above the subject line of the message, click on the small down arrow to the right of "Spam," and select "Report a Phishing Scam" from the menu.

Here are instructions on how to report fraudulent websites in popular browsers:

Google Chrome: Click on the icon at the top right that looks like a stack of three thick lines ("Customize and control Google Chrome"), then click on "Help", and "Report an Issue."

Microsoft Edge: Click on the icon at the top right that looks like three dots ("More"), then click on "Send Feedback." On the menu that appears, select "Report unsafe site."

Microsoft Internet Explorer 11: Click on the Gear icon ("Tools") at the top right of the screen, select "Safety," and then click on "Report unsafe website."

Mozilla Firefox: Click on the icon at the top right that looks like a stack of three thick lines ("Open menu"), then click on the question mark icon at the bottom ("Open Help Menu"). In the menu that appears, click on "Report Web Forgery."

Last of all, delete the phishing email!

Quick Reference Guide

If you see one, a few, or many of the following elements in an email, it is evidence that the message is likely a phishing scam.

<u>From: field:</u>

- Misspelled domain names
- Misspelled sender's name
- Improper capitalization
- Domain names that do not match the supposed seller
- Gibberish in the email address
- Unknown senders
- Other discrepancies

<u>To: field:</u>

- Multiple recipients
- Unrelated recipients
- Odd groupings of recipients

<u>Attachments:</u>

- Email attachments you are not expecting to receive

- Files which appear to have double extensions (like photo.jpg.exe)

Subject line:

- Subjects which convey a sense of urgency
- Subjects which try to scare us or tempt us with something illicit
- Subject lines which don't match the content of the message
- Strange wording, poor grammar, misspellings, and odd capitalization
- Emails which appear to be replies to messages we never sent

Contents:

- Emails which are blank except for a link or an attachment
- Business emails which are not personalized
- Strange wording, poor grammar, and misspellings
- Odd capitalization and inappropriate punctuation
- Threats
- Appeals to emotions such as greed, fear, or curiosity

Hyperlinks:

- Addresses within the link which don't match the message
- Misspelled domain names
- Anything suspicious

Basically, if something about the message doesn't look or feel right, don't trust it.

Glossary

APWG: The Anti-Phishing Working Group, a private international organization with members from the private and public sectors, including internet service providers, security companies, government agencies, and others. Its website may be found at www.antiphishing.org.

Attachment: A document, photo, or other computer file which is included with an email. Attachments are typically shown in email programs with a paperclip icon.

bcc: Blind carbon copy. This field in an email is used to add recipients to the message without others who receive the message being able to see that they were included.

cc: Carbon copy. This field in an email is used to add recipients to the message who are shown as receiving a copy of the message, rather than being included as direct recipients in the To: field.

Client: A computer program (such as an email program) which obtains information from another program or computer (called a server).

Clone phishing: A scheme in which a previously-sent email is copied and sent again to the same recipients by a scammer posing as the original sender, with the hyperlinks or attachments from the original message being replaced with fraudulent ones. This is an attempt to lull the recipients into a false sense of security, to get them to click on the link or open the attachment, ultimately to infect their computer with malware or to get them to fall victim to a fraud of some kind.

Domain name: The part of an email address which identifies the email service or other organization which hosts the email account or operates the internet site. It is the information after the @ symbol, typically formatted as a name followed by a period and a suffix (for example, microsoft.com).

Extension: The part of a file name at the very end after the period, typically three letters (such as .doc, .xls, .txt, .jpg, .pdf, etc.) It indicates the type of the file.

FBI: The U.S. Federal Bureau of Investigation.

From: The field in an email which is supposed to identify the name and email address of the sender. Unfortunately, the information in this field can be faked.

FTC: The U.S. Federal Trade Commission. Its mission is to "protect consumers and promote competition." Its website may be found at www.ftc.gov.

HIPAA: The Health Insurance Portability and Accountability Act. This is U.S. federal legislation governing data privacy and the security of personal health information. Details can be found at www.hhs.gov/hipaa/.

Hyperlink: An internet address you can click on that will take you to a website, download a document, or start a program.

IC3: The Internet Crime Complaint Center of the U.S. Federal Bureau of Investigation. It serves as a clearinghouse for reports of internet crimes, including phishing schemes. It reviews complaints and forwards them on to other agencies for appropriate action. Its website is at www.ic3.gov.

Identity theft: A crime where a thief steals information relating to another person, such as a social security number, bank account details, etc., and uses that information to impersonate the victim or otherwise defraud the victim or others, for the purpose of financial or other gain. Resources for reporting identity theft and developing a recovery plan are available at www.identitytheft.gov.

IRS: The U.S. Internal Revenue Service.

IT: Information Technology. In a company, the IT Department is the one which handles the computer hardware and software needs of the business.

Link: See *hyperlink*.

Malware: Software designed for malicious purposes, such as theft, spying, or destruction.

Phishing: A criminal scheme in which an email which appears to be from a reputable source is used to trick the email recipient into revealing valuable information to be used for theft, fraud or other illicit purposes.

Pretexting: Fraudulently obtaining confidential information from a person by making false statements.

Server: A computer system or program which holds and manages information centrally for access by other systems or programs. See also *client*.

Smishing: A phishing scheme conducted through the use of text messages (SMS) instead of emails.

SMS: Short Message Service. The official name for the cell phone text messaging system used universally.

Social engineering: A technique used by hackers and other criminals to obtain information about a person, an organization, or its computer network through the use of basic social skills and psychological manipulation.

Spear phishing: Highly-targeted phishing attacks customized with specific information about an individual or organization.

Spoofed: A fake. For example, a spoofed website is a copy that was made without permission, typically for fraudulent purposes. Similarly, a spoofed email appears to come from a sender other than the person who actually sent it.

Subject line: The field in an email where the sender can type a brief description of what the email is about, or some other wording designed to entice the recipient into opening the message.

To: The field in an email which shows the name and email address of the recipient or recipients of the message who were selected to be shown as receiving the message directly, rather than as a copy.

US-CERT: The United States Computer Emergency Readiness Team. It is a part of the National Cybersecurity and Communications Integration Center of the U.S. Department of Homeland Security. It collects and distributes information about internet threats. Its website may be found at www.us-cert.gov.

Virus: A malicious computer program designed to hide itself within other programs or data, which when run will damage or destroy data or perform other harmful tasks, while also making copies of itself to inject into other programs or computers, multiplying itself further.

Vishing: A phishing scheme conducted through the use of a voice telephone call instead of exclusively by email.

Whaling: A spear phishing attack directed to senior executives or celebrities using careful research.

Sources

Chapter One – What is Phishing?

Binational Working Group on Cross-Border Mass Marketing Fraud, "Report on Phishing: A Report to the Minister of Public Safety and Emergency Preparedness Canada and the Attorney General of the United States," October 2006, http://www.justice.gov/archive/opa/docs/report_on_phishing.pdf.

Burch, Greg; Grant, David; Harrell, David; and Taylor, Adrian, "Hackers Continue to Perpetrate Wire Transfer Fraud Scams on a Global Scale," JD Supra Business Advisor, September 14, 2015, http://www.jdsupra.com/legalnews/hackers-continue-to-perpetrate-wire-76144/.

Chang, Ellen, "Fraudsters Targeting New EMV Chip Credit Cards," TheStreet, October 22, 2015, http://www.thestreet.com/story/13334433/1/fraudsters-targeting-new-emv-chip-credit-cards.html.

DynaSis, "Hacking the 'Big Boys'–Small Businesses Become Pawns," January 19, 2016, http://www.dynasis.com/2016 /01/hacking-the-big-boys-small-businesses-become-pawns.

Federal Bureau of Investigation Internet Crime Complaint Center (IC3), "Internet Crime Schemes: Phishing/Spoofing," http://www.ic3.gov/crimeschemes.aspx.

Hooker, Thom, "Spear phishing and whaling attacks on the rise!", SMX Blog, September 4, 2015, http://smxemail.com/ spear-phishing-and-whaling-attacks-on-the-rise.html.

Lord, Nate, "Social Engineering Attacks: Common Techniques & How to Prevent an Attack," Digital Guardian, November 6, 2015, https://digitalguardian.com/blog/social-engineering-attacks-common-techniques-how-prevent-attack.

McMillan, David, "The perils of phishing: How cybercriminals are targeting your weakest link," IBM X-Force Research, 2015, http://public.dhe.ibm.com/common/ssi/ecm/se/en/ sel03033usen/SEL03033USEN.PDF.

Olavsrud, Thor, "11 Steps Attackers Took to Crack Target," CIO, September 2, 2014, http://www.cio.com/article/ 2600345/security0/11-steps-attackers-took-to-crack-target.html.

PayPal, "Recognize fraudulent emails and websites," http://www.paypal.com/us/webapps/mpp/security/ suspicious-activity.

Perlroth, Nicole, and Harris, Elizabeth A., "Cyberattack Insurance a Challenge for Business," New York Times, June 8, 2014, http://www.nytimes.com/2014/06/09/business/ cyberattack-insurance-a-challenge-for-business.html.

Toppol, Omri, "Nigerian Email Scam, Phishing Attacks &
More: Beware of Your Inbox," LogDog Blog, May 20, 2015,
http://getlogdog.com/blogdog/nigerian-email-scam-phishing-
attacks-more-beware-of-your-inbox/.

United States Computer Emergency Readiness Team, National
Cybersecurity and Communications Integration Center,
"Security Tip (ST04-014): Avoiding Social Engineering and
Phishing Attacks," February 6, 2013, https://www.us-
cert.gov/ ncas/tips/ST04-014.

Chapter Two – Is Phishing a Serious Problem?

Aguilar, Mario, "The Number of People Who Fall for Phishing
Emails Is Staggering," Gizmodo, April 15, 2015,
http://gizmodo.com/the-number-of-people-who-fall-for-
phishing-emails-is-st-1697725476.

Association of Corporate Counsel, *Workplace Information Risk in
the Digital Age: Monitoring Employees, Social Media Challenges,
Managing Access to Data, and Optimizing Flexibility* (InfoPak),
February 2014.

Bisson, David, "Sony Hackers Used Phishing Emails to Breach
Company Networks," Tripwire, April 22, 2015,
http://www.tripwire.com/state-of-security/latest-security-
news/sony-hackers-used-phishing-emails-to-breach-company-
networks/.

Bowman, Dan, "Report: Healthcare more susceptible to
privacy attacks than other industries," FierceHealthIT,
September 25, 2015, https://www.fiercehealthit.com/

story/report-healthcare-more-susceptible-privacy-attacks-other-industries/2015-09-25.

Brownlee, Lisa, "Simulated Phishing Attacks Yield 37 Percent Return on Investment," Forbes, October 7, 2015, http://www.forbes.com/sites/lisabrownlee/2015/10/07/security-simulated-phishing-attacks-yield-37-percent-return-on-investment/.

Buckley, Sean, "Google says the best phishing scams have a 45-percent success rate," Engadget, November 8, 2014, http://www.engadget.com/2014/11/08/google-says-the-best-phishing-scams-have-a-45-percent-success-r/

Chaitin, Daniel, "25% of postal service workers fall victim to scam emails," Washington Examiner, October 10, 2015, http://www.washingtonexaminer.com/25-of-postal-service-workers-fall-victim-to-scam-emails/article/2573843.

Chmielewski, Dawn, "Sony Begins to Tally Its Financial Loss from Hack: $15 Million and Counting," Recode, February 4, 2015, http://recode.net/2015/02/04/sony-begins-to-tally-its-financial-loss-from-hack-15-million-and-counting/.

Federal Bureau of Investigation, "Georgia Man Convicted in New Jersey for His Role in Phishing Scheme" (press release), June 27, 2012, https://www.fbi.gov/newark/press-releases/2012/georgia-man-convicted-in-new-jersey-for-his-role-in-phishing-scheme.

Federal Trade Commission, "Enforcing Privacy Promises," https://www.ftc.gov/news-events/media-resources/protecting-consumer-privacy/enforcing-privacy-promises.

Gent, Edd, "Phishing emails averaging at 20 a month, research reveals," Engineering & Technology Magazine, August 20, 2015, http://eandt.theiet.org/news/2015/aug/phishing-attacks.cfm.

Krebs, Brian, "Seagate Phish Exposes All Employee W-2's," KrebsOnSecurity, March 16, 2016, http://krebsonsecurity.com/2016/03/seagate-phish-exposes-all-employee-w-2s/.

Lord, Nate, "Social Engineering Attacks: Common Techniques & How to Prevent an Attack," Digital Guardian, November 6, 2015, https://digitalguardian.com/blog/social-engineering-attacks-common-techniques-how-prevent-attack.

Mandak, Joe, "Moldovan phishing scheme took $3.5M from drilling accounts," Associated Press, October 14, 2015, http://bigstory.ap.org/article/8c8160dc9a9449e8a962e6531e60311c/moldovan-bank-phishing-scheme-cost-drilling-firm-35m.

McGee, Marianne Kolbasuk, "Phishing Breach Results in $750,000 HIPAA Penalty," Data Breach Today, December 14, 2015, http://www.databreachtoday.com/phishing-breach-results-in-750000-hipaa-penalty-a-8747.

Miller, Chance, "Man behind celebrity nude photos leaked from iCloud pleads guilty to phishing scheme," 9to5Mac.com, March 15, 2016, http://9to5mac.com/2016/03/15/celebrity-icloud-nude-photos-leak-hacker-charged/.

Milton Security Group, "Oldham Schools Data Breach Affects 2,800," Milton Security Information Security Blog, September 28, 2015, http://www.miltonstart.com/blog/2015/09/28/oldham-schools-data-breach-affects-2800/.

Mogg, Trevor, "Hollywood Hospital Pays $17,000 To Ransomware Hackers," Digital Trends, February 18, 2016, http://www.digitaltrends.com/computing/hollywood-hospital-ransomware-attack.

Petterson, Edvard, "Sony to Pay as Much as $8 Million to Settle Data-Breach Case," Bloomberg, October 20, 2015, http://www.bloomberg.com/news/articles/2015-10-20/sony-to-pay-as-much-as-8-million-to-settle-data-breach-claims.

Practical Law Company, "Breach Notification" (Practice Note), accessed October 28, 2015, http://us.practicallaw.com/3-501-1474.

Practical Law Company, "Cyber Attacks: Prevention and Proactive Responses" (Practice Note), accessed October 28, 2015, http://us.practicallaw.com/3-511-5848.

Practical Law Company, "How Safe Is Your Company's Intellectual Property from Cyber Attack?" (Legal Update), October 27, 2015, http://us.practicallaw.com/w-000-7122.

Public Safety Canada, "Phishing: How many take the bait?" (infographic), http://www.getcybersafe.gc.ca/cnt/rsrcs/nfgrphcs/nfgrphcs-2012-10-11-en.aspx.

ThreatSim, *State of the Phish 2015* (report).

Chapter Four – Who is Sending the Email?

Tompor, Susan, "Beware this phishing e-mail tax scam from 'the boss'," Detroit Free Press, March 8, 2016, http://www.freep.com/story/money/personal-finance/susan-tompor/2016/03/05/w-2-phishing-scam-tax-id-fraud/81214316/.

Chapter Seven – What is the Subject Line of the Email?

Brent, Douglas F., " 'Are You at Your Desk?' The Simple Swindle that's Harming Companies During Tax Season," Lexology, March 11, 2016, http://www.lexology.com/library/detail.aspx?g=c0c18040-7352-4a37-973c-0ac53175447f.

Chapter Eight – What Does the Email Say?

Binational Working Group on Cross-Border Mass Marketing Fraud, "Report on Phishing: A Report to the Minister of Public Safety and Emergency Preparedness Canada and the Attorney General of the United States," October 2006, http://www.justice.gov/archive/opa/docs/report_on_phishing.pdf.

Erb, Kelly Phillips, "It's Not A Scam: IRS Is Really Sending Out Identity Verification Letters," Forbes, March 18, 2015, http://www.forbes.com/sites/kellyphillipserb/2015/03/18/its-not-a-scam-irs-is-really-sending-out-identity-verification-letters.

Federal Bureau of Investigation, "Spam E-Mails Continuing to Capitalize on FBI Officials' Names," September 25, 2013, http://www.ic3.gov/media/2013/130925.aspx.

Federal Trade Commission, *Protecting Personal Information: A Guide for Business*, November 2011, https://www.ftc.gov/

system/files/documents/plain-language/bus69-protecting-personal-information-guide-business_0.pdf.

Lord, Nate, "Social Engineering Attacks: Common Techniques & How to Prevent an Attack," Digital Guardian, November 6, 2015, https://digitalguardian.com/blog/social-engineering-attacks-common-techniques-how-prevent-attack.

Mandak, Joe, "Moldovan phishing scheme took $3.5M from drilling accounts," Associated Press, October 14, 2015, http://bigstory.ap.org/article/8c8160dc9a9449e8a962e6531e60311c/moldovan-bank-phishing-scheme-cost-drilling-firm-35m.

PhishingBox, "Types of Phishing Defined," April 16, 2013, http://www.phishingbox.com/types-of-phishing-defined/.

University of Washington, Office of the Chief Information Security Officer, *Information Security and Privacy Risk Advisory: Phishing*, February 2011, https://ciso.uw.edu/site/files/risk_advisory_phishing.pdf.

Chapter Ten – So What Do I Do with This Phishing Email?

ADP, "Protection Against Phishing," http://www.adp.com/who-we-are/data-security-and-privacy/protection-against-phishing.aspx.

Anti-Phishing Working Group, "About the APWG: Charter and Saga," http://www.antiphishing.org/about-APWG/APWG/.

Apple, "Identifying fraudulent 'phishing' email," June 1, 2015, https://support.apple.com/en-us/HT204759.

Apple, "Phishing & Other Suspicious Emails," http://www.apple.com/legal/more-resources/phishing/.

Bank of America, "Report a Suspicious Email," https://www.bankofamerica.com/privacy/report-suspicious-email.go.

Better Business Bureau, "ALERT: Phishing Scam Looks Like BBB Email...But It's Not," https://www.bbb.org/council/about/alert-phishing-scam-looks-like-bbb-emailbut-its-not/.

Chase Bank, "How to Report Fraud," https://www.chase.com/digital/resources/privacy-security/security/report-fraud.

Dropbox, "How can I stay protected from phishing and malware?", https://www.dropbox.com/help/9113.

Ebay, "How do I report emails that might be fake (spoof)?", http://pages.ebay.com/help/account/questions/report-spoof-email.html.

Federal Bureau of Investigation Internet Crime Complaint Center, "Frequently Asked Questions," http://www.ic3.gov/faq/default.aspx.

Federal Trade Commission, "FTC Unveils New E-mail Address for Deceptive Spam: Spam@uce.gov" (press release), July 28, 2004, https://www.ftc.gov/news-events/press-releases/2004/07/ftc-unveils-new-e-mail-address-deceptive-spam-spamucegov.

Federal Trade Commission, "Phishing," https://www.consumer.ftc.gov/articles/0003-phishing.

Financial Fraud Enforcement Task Force, "Report Financial Fraud," http://www.stopfraud.gov/report.html.

Google, "Avoid and report Google scams," https://support.google.com/faqs/answer/2952493.

Google, "Making the Web Safer," https://www.google.com/transparencyreport/safebrowsing/.

Internal Revenue Service, "Report Phishing and Online Scams," February 3, 2016, https://www.irs.gov/uac/Report-Phishing.

Microsoft TechNet, "Submit spam, non-spam, and phishing scam messages to Microsoft for analysis," https://technet.microsoft.com/en-us/library/jj200769(v=exchg.150).aspx.

Microsoft, "Email and web scams: How to help protect yourself," https://www.microsoft.com/en-us/security/online-privacy/phishing-scams.aspx.

PayPal, "Report a suspicious email or website," https://www.paypal.com/us/webapps/mpp/security/report-problem.

Practical Law Company, "Cyber Attacks: Prevention and Proactive Responses" (Practice Note), accessed October 28, 2015, http://us.practicallaw.com/3-511-5848.

University of Washington, Office of the Chief Information Security Officer, *Information Security and Privacy Risk Advisory:*

Phishing, February 2011, https://ciso.uw.edu/site/
files/risk_advisory_phishing.pdf.

Verizon, "Report a Security Vulnerability,"
http://www.verizon.com/info/reportphishing/?c=2.

Wells Fargo, "How to Report Phish and Email Scams,"
https://www.wellsfargo.com/privacy-security/fraud/
report/phish/.

United States Computer Emergency Readiness Team, National
Cybersecurity and Communications Integration Center,
"Report Phishing Scams," https://www.us-cert.gov/report-
phishing.

Glossary

Binational Working Group on Cross-Border Mass Marketing
Fraud, "Report on Phishing: A Report to the Minister of
Public Safety and Emergency Preparedness Canada and the
Attorney General of the United States," October 2006,
http://www.justice.gov/archive/opa/docs/report_on_
phishing.pdf.

Department of Health and Human Services, "Health
Information Privacy," http://www.hhs.gov/hipaa/.

Department of Justice, "Identity Theft," November 2, 2015,
https://www.justice.gov/criminal-fraud/identity-theft/
identity-theft-and-identity-fraud.

Federal Bureau of Investigation Internet Crime Complaint
Center (IC3), "Internet Crime Schemes: Phishing/Spoofing,"
http://www.ic3.gov/crimeschemes.aspx.

Federal Trade Commission, "About the FTC: What We Do," https://www.ftc.gov/about-ftc/what-we-do.

Federal Trade Commission, "Recovering from Identity Theft," https://www.consumer.ftc.gov/features/feature-0014-identity-theft.

McMillan, David, "The perils of phishing: How cybercriminals are targeting your weakest link," IBM X-Force Research, 2015, http://public.dhe.ibm.com/common/ssi/ecm/se/en/sel03033usen/SEL03033USEN.PDF.

PC Magazine Encyclopedia, "SMS," http://www.pcmag.com/encyclopedia/term/51563/sms.

PC Magazine Encyclopedia, "Virus," http://www.pcmag.com/encyclopedia/term/53963/virus.

PhishingBox, "Types of Phishing Defined," April 16, 2013, http://www.phishingbox.com/types-of-phishing-defined/.

Practical Law Company, "Cyber Attacks: Prevention and Proactive Responses" (Practice Note), accessed October 28, 2015, http://us.practicallaw.com/3-511-5848.

United States Computer Emergency Readiness Team, National Cybersecurity and Communications Integration Center, "About Us," https://www.us-cert.gov/about-us.

United States Computer Emergency Readiness Team, National Cybersecurity and Communications Integration Center, "Security Tip (ST04-014): Avoiding Social Engineering and Phishing Attacks," February 6, 2013, https://www.us-cert.gov/ncas/tips/ST04-014.

University of Washington, Office of the Chief Information Security Officer, *Information Security and Privacy Risk Advisory: Phishing*, February 2011, https://ciso.uw.edu/site/ files/risk_advisory_phishing.pdf.

ABOUT THE AUTHOR

Brett W. Smith is a native of Jacksonville, Florida. He studied math and government at the University of Texas at Austin, and political science, accounting, and German at Brigham Young University. After graduating from law school at BYU, he became an attorney, working both in private practice and in corporate legal departments.

He has also worked as computer network administrator and database administrator. He has been fascinated by computers and software since getting his first computer in college, an IBM PC-XT. Its 10 MB hard disk seemed to be immense.

Although he is an attorney, he dislikes legalese and prefers plain English. He focuses on making complex topics more understandable.

He now resides in Spokane, Washington.